MIX
Papier aus verantwortungsvollen Quellen
Paper from responsible sources
FSC® C105338

Roger Edwards

An Investigation into the Use of Social Networking Sites by Young People and the Perceived Benefits

Anchor Academic Publishing

Edwards, Roger: An Investigation into the Use of Social Networking Sites by Young People and the Perceived Benefits, Hamburg, Anchor Academic Publishing 2017

Buch-ISBN: 978-3-95489-474-1
PDF-eBook-ISBN: 978-3-95489-401-7
Druck/Herstellung: Anchor Academic Publishing, Hamburg, 2017

Bibliografische Information der Deutschen Nationalbibliothek:
Die Deutsche Nationalbibliothek verzeichnet diese Publikation in der Deutschen Nationalbibliografie; detaillierte bibliografische Daten sind im Internet über http://dnb.d-nb.de abrufbar.

Bibliographical Information of the German National Library:
The German National Library lists this publication in the German National Bibliography. Detailed bibliographic data can be found at: http://dnb.d-nb.de

All rights reserved. This publication may not be reproduced, stored in a retrieval system or transmitted, in any form or by any means, electronic, mechanical, photocopying, recording or otherwise, without the prior permission of the publishers.

Das Werk einschließlich aller seiner Teile ist urheberrechtlich geschützt. Jede Verwertung außerhalb der Grenzen des Urheberrechtsgesetzes ist ohne Zustimmung des Verlages unzulässig und strafbar. Dies gilt insbesondere für Vervielfältigungen, Übersetzungen, Mikroverfilmungen und die Einspeicherung und Bearbeitung in elektronischen Systemen.

Die Wiedergabe von Gebrauchsnamen, Handelsnamen, Warenbezeichnungen usw. in diesem Werk berechtigt auch ohne besondere Kennzeichnung nicht zu der Annahme, dass solche Namen im Sinne der Warenzeichen- und Markenschutz-Gesetzgebung als frei zu betrachten wären und daher von jedermann benutzt werden dürften.

Die Informationen in diesem Werk wurden mit Sorgfalt erarbeitet. Dennoch können Fehler nicht vollständig ausgeschlossen werden und die Diplomica Verlag GmbH, die Autoren oder Übersetzer übernehmen keine juristische Verantwortung oder irgendeine Haftung für evtl. verbliebene fehlerhafte Angaben und deren Folgen.

Alle Rechte vorbehalten

© Anchor Academic Publishing, Imprint der Diplomica Verlag GmbH
Hermannstal 119k, 22119 Hamburg
http://www.diplomica-verlag.de, Hamburg 2017
Printed in Germany

TABLE OF CONTENTS

ABSTRACT ....Page 2

CHAPTER 1: INTRODUCTION ....Page 3-5

CHAPTER 2: LITERATURE REVIEW..Page 6-9

CHAPTER 3: METHODOLOGY..Page 10-15

CHAPTER 4: RESULTS AND DISCUSSION...Page 16-24

CHAPTER 5: CONCLUSION ....Page 25-26

APPENDIX A – GLOSSARY OF KEY TERMS...Page 27-29

REFERENCES ....Page 30-38

ABSTRACT

The use of social networking sites (SNS) has been adopted and integrated into the daily lives of an increasing number of adolescents and young people overall are amongst its most prolific and substantial users. This study discuss a number of issues related to the use of social media and social networking sites such as; why do young people mass to such sites? What do young people express on these SNS? And lastly, how do these sites enhance or fit into the lives of young people? Much has been said regarding the risk management paradigm with regards to social media use by young people therefore this study attempts to readdress this imbalance and focus on the perceived benefits; however it did not ignore the potential contents and contact risk which was also explored. This study found that there are a number of significant benefits associated with the use of SNS including: enhanced learning opportunities; facilitating supportive relationships; identity formation; not to mention its contribution towards the emotional, psychological and social wellbeing of young people.

CHAPTER 1: INTRODUCTION

(NB. A glossary of terms used in this study is presented in Appendix A to assist the reader.)

In recent years, online social networking Sites (SNS) have become integrated into our everyday lives and young people in particular are amongst it's most prolific and substantial users (Boyd 2010). Recent studies (Madden et al., 2013) have found that 95 % of young people (aged 12 to 17) use the internet and 81 % are users of social network sites. According to The Pew Research Center's Internet & American Life Teen-Parent survey, (2012) *Facebook* secured 94 % of all social media networking teens, *Twitter* 26% and *Instagram* 11%.

Based on this prevalent use, SNS and in particular *Facebook* (which by the end of 2013, reported to have 1.23 billion users – Kiss (2014)) have potentially significant implications on the daily lives of adolescents and raises some very important questions, such as; why do young people mass to such sites? What do young people express on these SNS? And lastly, how do these sites enhance or fit into the lives of young people?

The goal of this study is to address the aforementioned questions and explore some of the implications on the lives of young people. Before an explanation is given on the rationale behind the topic of research, it's important to understand the key features of social networking sites and equally a number of considerations which structure this study.

Firstly, Social networking sites (SNS) as defined by Boyd and Ellison (2007) are *"web-based services that allow individuals to (1) construct a public or semi-public profile within a bounded system, (2) articulate a list of other users with whom they share a connection, and (3) view and traverse their list of connections and those made by others within the system. The nature and nomenclature of these connections may vary from site to site"* (p210-230).

Social networking sites (SNS) include social media sites such as *Facebook, MySpace, Twitter* and *Instagram* to name a few. Equally, according to Boyd and Ellison (2008) many other web based sites which were developed for media sharing (i.e. *YouTube, Tumblr, Pinterest, Last FM* etc.) have also incorporated a profile feature and may also come under the umbrella of SNS. For purpose of this study, it must be noted that this paper will focus on the Facebook social networking site.

Inextricably linked to the phrase *'social networking'* is the term *'social media'* which refers to the technology and online social instruments of communication that allow interactive community based content sharing and collaboration. For example; online chatrooms / forums, microblogging, podcasts, social networking sites and wikis. (See Appendix A.) Throughout this research the term young people, teens/teenagers and adolescents are used interchangeably. It is however challenging to define the aforementioned terms since there are no universally accepted definitions. In most cases these terms/labels are socially and culturally created (Ito et al. 2009). Nevertheless the United Nations and the World Health Organization define adolescents to include persons aged 10-19 years and youth between 15-24. Together, adolescents and youth are referred to as young people aged 10-24. Given this broad variance my focus will be on the research carried out on persons aged between 12-18.

I will however consider pertinent research on the young adult population (i.e. college/university students) as this is the field that is most prevalent currently. Indeed research literature on young people aged 12-18 is only recently emerging as a major focal point. Nonetheless, existing and more well-established research on the young adult population will undoubtedly yield a rich theoretical structure which will conceptualised and provide context for the adolescent/teen population. The implication for me is considering whether such findings are applicable to the younger subject audience and identifying where there might be possible discrepancies between them and the older group.

Early (and most) research literature on SNS and social media focuses primarily on the risk management paradigm and discourse (Wolak et al 2006; 2008, Aoyama & Talbert 2010, Call & Burrow-Sanchez 2010). Thus the main purpose of this study is to investigate and illuminate the benefits connected to SNS use by young people, which to date has been neglected in public debate. I will endeavour to endorse and summarise young people's opinions on the subject, considering they are often the most proficient users of social media and new technology.

As adults we often view young people or adolescents as a developmental stage of what ultimately they will become and not essentially as a complete being (Corsaro 1997). As such most of the studies in this territory have neglected the adolescent population and are from an adult standpoint rather than a youth centred approach which acknowledges young people as actors in their own social world (James and Prout 1997).

As a Pastoral Head of Year working within a secondary school; I often have to deal with the remnants of some of the social disputes on SNS such as cyber-bullying, sexting etc. (See appendix A.) As a result, this has had an adverse effect on my opinion with regard to the benefits of SNS and the impact it has on the lives of young people. Undoubtedly, dealing with these concerns has strengthened my alignment with the discourse that is echoed and magnified by the adult population regarding the use of SNS by young people and the associated risks. Therefore further exploration of this topic will allow me to readdress the imbalance within my work practice and in turn will enhance my professional development and knowledge.

CHAPTER 2: LITERATURE REVIEW

It is essential to investigate what other scholars have written in relation to this topic and for this purpose, this literature review has been produced to summarise existing knowledge and to provide a contextual background. Kumar (2012) argues that it is an essential preliminary task which makes a valuable contribution to every operational step and provides a valuable insight into the theoretical roots and research methodology of a research topic. He also states that *"Later in the process, the literature review serves to enhance and consolidate your own knowledge base and helps you to integrate your findings with the existing body of knowledge. Since an important responsibility in research is to compare your findings with those of others, it is here that the literature review plays an extremely important role"*. (Kumar 2012; p 51)

Firstly, there is the rapidly increasing body of empirical research exploring how young people create social network profiles and the different types of interaction that occurs between the different networks (Donath and Boyd 2004; Boyd and Ellison, 2007; Hinduja and Patching, in press; Lenhart and Madden, 2007).

Moreover ethnographic data from Boyd's 2007 two year study; found that young people use SNS to express different aspect of themselves both as individuals and as part of a group. This viewpoint has also been endorsed by Livingstone (2008) and Ito et al. (2009). Equally, Boyd (2007) and Watkins (2009) found that despite the potential for global networking, young people uses SNS to connect with friends in their local network and their online personal and social identity is endorsed by comments or *'likes'* from other young people in their network. (See Appendix A.)

Therefore a hypothesis underpinning this study is that the attitudes, perceptions, behaviours and interaction on these SNS have a set of social and technical affordances that have the potential to affect, shape and negotiate the social and personal identity of young people. For example, research conducted by Walther et al. (2008) found that friends' input including, dialogue/conversation and photos, on one's social media profile are all seen by others as indicators of one's identity as much as one's own comments. Such findings demonstrate the complexity of identity processes and indicators.

According to Tajfel (1978) and Tajfel & Turner (1986); Social identity is a person's sense of who they are; based on similarities and differences with others. Our social identity provides a basis for shared social action and attitudes; it provides social validation, self-understanding /clarification, expression and relationship development. Harwood (2006) suggests that social identity is experienced in a variety of group settings such as demographic factors, and cultural, family and peer groups.

Similarly the concepts of reciprocity and deindividualization (NB. see Appendix A) are important facets in understanding adolescent social identity because adolescent development is characterized by sense of enhanced and frequent modification to social norms (Waterman & Archer 1990). It is a period in which social networks and friendship/relationship formation become extremely important to the construction of social and personal identity and behaviour (Giordano, 2003; Mesch 2010). What SNS provide are new ways and opportunities for young people to shape and navigate their social environment, make sense of cultural cues, grapple with social norms, explore new interests and forms of self-expression/identity coupled with enhancing their technological skills. In a similar fashion, Jenkins (2006) and Ito et al. (2008; 2009) argue that if young people are not able to access these online communities, then they may not develop the necessary skills and technical/media literacy. Thus these online communities are now fixtures of youth culture and provide a platform for self-directed learning, autonomy, bolstering technical skills and refining socio-emotional skills; so that young people can fully participate in contemporary society (Ito et al. 2008; 2009).

Two related strands of research inextricably linked to the topic of social networking profiles and the nature and use of the different types of interaction are social capital / capital gain (NB. see Appendix A) and online/offline interaction. Previous research has documented a relationship between the use of SNS and increased levels of social capital/support and reciprocity (Wellman et al 1996). Equally the perceived value of online interaction is echoed by findings from the PEW study (Lenhart et al 2001). They found that online communication added value to existing friendship for young people (offering advice, assistance with school work, access to news and currents events etc) and did not affect or reduce or displace face to face interaction. Livingstone (2008) echoed similar findings and found that despite the fact SNS may have displaced other forms of online communication (i.e. email, chatrooms, etc.), it incorporates others (i.e. instant messaging, blogging, media sharing etc.) and remediates additional face to face and telephone communication. Furthermore the literature on personal relations and the social capital hypothesis has gone as far as to suggest that SNS such as Facebook provide resources and a forum to build self efficacy through a supportive network of friends (Ellison et al 2007; 2008). It also consolidates social relationships and communities (through *'Fan/Group Page'*), enhances creativity (i.e. young people becomes producer of media) , promotes self and collective expression/identity, promotes greater school involvement and work ethic and provides formal and informal educational outcomes (Anderson 2007; Mazer et al 2007; Notley 2010; Ito et al 2008;2013). Lastly, there is also the proposition that it promotes national/global awareness and civic and political participation (as in the case of KONY 2012 | Invisible Children).

Other supporters of the social capital and psychological wellbeing hypothesis include Steinfield et al. (2007; 2008) and Valenzuela et al. (2009). However, it is worth noting, that most of this research was conducted on college students and not adolescent youth. Nonetheless there is an extensive body of ethnographic studies conducted by Ito et al. (2008; 2009) examining youth media practices of young people. In their research they found that young people engage in three genres of participation, (i.e. *'Hanging Out, Messing Around, and Geeking Out'*) that describe different forms of commitment to media engagement and correspond to different social and learning dynamics.

'Hanging Out' relates to friendship-driven practices; in particular, the use SNS to spend casual social time with each other. The exploration of new interests and information outside the young person's immediate network refers to the *'Messing Around'* genre of participation. This allows young people to connect to others and share particular interests (i.e. online gaming, podcasting, video blogging etc) which may result in acquiring new technical and media literacy skills. *'Geeking Out'* refers to the thirst for specialised knowledge and enhanced status among expert peers through self directed means; such as sharing knowledge over forums/chatrooms, social gaming groups and illegal downloads (of music, software and films through the use of peer-to-peer file-sharing software such as *'Torrent'*). *'Geeking Out'* incorporates adult participation however adults are not necessary the specialist by means of age and as such *'Geeking Out'* destroys the conventional indicators of status and power.

Additionally, it is worth noting that social capital is a theoretical concept which originates from the works of Bourdieu (1986) and Coleman (1988). According to Ellison et al (2010) citing Putman (2000), *"social capital refers to the benefits that can be attained from connections between people through social networks."*

To provide further contextual background and a unified theoretical framework for this paper, it is also worth considering the wider volume of research examining adolescent cognitive and psychological Development. Developmental theorists such as Erikson (1968; 1970) and Marcia (1966; 1976; 1980) provide a framework for thinking about human growth, development, and learning.

Another spectrum of research linked to the topic of social identity, which we looked at earlier in this chapter, is the issue of personal identity. Buckingham (2008, p1) expressed that identity, like adolescence, is *"an ambiguous and slippery term"*. However for the purpose of this study; by personal identity we mean how one perceives oneself and how others perceive one in the larger social environment. Both social identity and personal identity are inextricably linked and Deaux (1992) articulates that our role within the wider social context can affect and motivate our personal values and beliefs, how we view ourselves, our behaviour and our choices of relationship. (For example, our gender, ethnicity, religion political affiliation etc.)

CHAPTER 3: METHODOLOGY

In this chapter I will discuss and describe the research methodology used in this study. A simple and general definition of the methodology is described as the systems of methods, overall approach or path used to find the answers to research question(s) (Leedy & Ormrod 2001; Kumar 2014). Within this chapter we will look at the philosophy that underpins the research approach and design, the method of research and describe and contrast the different research instruments/tools used to collect data, including the methods used to uphold validity and reliability of the instruments.

The approach in which research is conducted is conceived in terms of the research philosophy. The research philosophy is a conviction/belief about the way in which data should be collected, analysed and utilised regarding a phenomenon. There are two theoretical paradigms of thoughts regarding the philosophical approach to research; the positivist approach and the interpretivist approach (also known as the constructivist approach). Within the context of this study, I will pursue the interpretivist approach to answering the research questions posed.

The positivist approach seeks understanding based on systematic observation and research, by the aim of establishing social laws parallel to the natural laws; uncovered by the techniques of natural sciences (Marshall 1994). Early positivists such Auguste Comte and Emile Durkheim endorsed that an accurate and objective explanation of the cause of a social phenomena can only be identified and accessed via scientific standards of verification.

This approach further seeks to hypothesize and then assess fundamental presumptions/regularities or inductive reasoning about a social trend that can then be generalised (Lin 1998). Quantitative research (which we will look at later in this chapter) is inherently linked to the positivist concept with an emphasis on assembling and adapting data into numerical structures so that statistical analysis and conclusions can be drawn; the results of which are typically presented using statistics, tables and graphs etc. (ACAPS 2012).

Like Clark and Bell (2012, p115 in Bradford and Cullen) I share a sense of scepticism that social behaviour, and indeed the behaviour of young people using SNS, can be explained through such a restrictive and rigid approach that the positivist approach offers. This approach places significant importance to rationality, objectivity, prediction and control (Streubert and Carpenter, 1999: 7). Tucker (2012 p31 in Bradford and Cullen) citing the works of Becks (1979:141) argues that *"the purpose of social science is to understand social reality as different people see it and to demonstrate how their lives shape the action which they take within that reality"*. Fundamentally my research questions inherently endorse the interpretivist approach because of the many variables and the open minded nature of the questions posed.

The interpretivist approach seeks to understand how people interpret a phenomenon or event (Cohen & Manion, 1994, p.36), rather than an objective truth. It suggests that facts are, or reality is, socially constructed interpreted and subjective (Mertens, 2005, p.12). It acknowledges that there are many interpretations of reality including the researcher's own; thus research findings are jointly created or *'co-constructed'* with the participants (Ponterotto, 2005, p.129). The researcher's role is to unearth the different versions of reality within the specific context. This approach also upholds that these various interpretations of reality are in themselves an integral component of the scientific knowledge being pursued.

In comparison, qualitative research tends to be associated with the interpretivist / constructivist paradigm. Clark and Bell (2012, p115 in Bradford and Cullen) state that *"qualitative research upholds the idea that sociological enquiry, by its very nature, can only be interpretative and cannot aspire towards the generation of generalisable explanations of human and social behaviour."*

The aforementioned differences in the uses and subsequent inference that can be drawn from both philosophies have led conformists from both camps, to assert that these two approaches are diametrically opposed ways of conducting research (Lee 1991 p342). Whilst I shall not elaborate on this debate further, it is of my opinion that that interpretivist approach can facilitate the correct answers to the research question(s) posed and provide rich analysis of people's social world (Geertz 1973; 'thick *description'*) coupled with adding validity towards the conclusion. I do however acknowledge that only by methods of scientific deduction will I be able to assess and validate some of the hypothesis raised (King et al. 1994). So in essence, both research approaches are not necessarily at opposing ends but as Roth et al. (2002, p132) states *"require different analytical lenses for the same data."* Equally both approaches are valuable in different settings and in relation to particular research dilemmas. Significantly many scholars have endorsed the use of both approaches collectively, to ensure quality of research. (Kaplan and Duchon 1988; Lee 1991).

Similarly, a combination of different types and sources of data will be utilised in this study so that a holistic picture can be achieved. Sources of information will include both primary and secondary data and qualitative and quantitative data. Invariably there is an ongoing theme of a mixed method approach.

Researchers have to think about the sources on which to base and substantiate their research and findings. The choices available are between primary data and secondary sources. I will be using both; often referred to as triangulation, or dual methodology (i.e. combining primary and secondary data from qualitative and quantitative data; methodological/data triangulation).

The triangulation or dual methodology approach to research was developed by Webb et al. (1966) and extended by Denzin (1970). They argued that researchers should employ multiple instruments to measure variables, thus establishing validity in their work by analysing a research question from several angles.

The purpose for the utilisation of secondary data is mainly one of time constraint and financial restriction and equally as Hinds et al., 1997 (cited *in* Long-Sutehall et al., 2010 p336) suggest many researchers *"have applied secondary analysis to data when they have wanted to: pursue interests distinct to those of the original analysis"*. This point is a significant one, as there is a body of work currently available to tackle my research questions; namely Ellison et al 2007; Boyd 2007; Livingstone 2008; Stern 2008; Ito et al. 2009; not to mention the large volume of qualitative and quantitative data from Madden et al. 2013.

Long-Sutehall et al. 2010 states; "it is recommended that the research questions for the secondary analysis be sufficiently close to those of the primary research, but that the data collection and analytic techniques in the primary dataset are similar to those that will be applied in the secondary analysis." Equally my primary data will provide a platform to cross-validate and consolidate my results.

A simple definition of primary data is the data collected by the researcher themselves (i.e. via interviews, observations, questionnaires etc.) and secondary sources are data that already exist from previous research or enquiries (i.e. certified statistics, government reports/surveys, web information etc.).

As we have already discussed, quantitative research is represented as the conventional scientific approach to research that is underpinned in the philosophical paradigm acknowledged as positivism. According to Burns and Grove (2005:23)*"quantitative research is a formal, objective, systematic process in which numerical data are used to obtain information about the world"*. They add that *"this method is used to describe variables, examine relationships among variables and determine cause-effect interactions between variables."*

Another distinguishing aim of quantitative research is that it is often utilised to test a pre-determined hypotheses; thus there is a common perception that the emphasis is on proof rather than discovery. It utilises experiments, tests and surveys which may be presented in the format of structured interviews or questionnaires. This approach decontextualizes human behaviour and as a result, responses from such instruments would be primarily numerical and may lack explanation or depth (Geertz 1973; 'thick *description'*). However, the accuracy of the research design means that results can be objectively processed and the outcome can be quantified and subjected to statistical treatment in order to support or refute *"alternate knowledge claims"* (Creswell, 2003, p. 153). This suggests that the reliability and validity of research results also depends on cautious assessment of the conditions in which outcome measures were applied.

Qualitative research tends to be linked with the interpretivist paradigm of research principles with a focus on the social context of reality and words as the unit of analysis. Instrumental to this approach is finding out the deeper meaning and significance of peoples' behaviour and experiences through deploying research instruments such as an unstructured or semi-structured interviews, audio recordings and transcript, case studies, photographs etc. As most responses are verbal, you achieve a more in-depth explanation; however interpretation may prove challenging and subjective. Equally the narrative analysis may also be inconclusive. Davis (2007 p. 577) reminds us that *"even the most credible research is subject to differing interpretations and rarely depicts the final word or indispensable truth"*.

In summary, both qualitative and quantitative research method as lone entities are vulnerable, however used in combination can consolidate each other and provide validity to each other's findings; hence my motive for utilising both.

For this study I will re-evaluate the findings collated by Ito et al. (2009) which is rich in qualitative data such as diary studies, semi structured interviews, focus groups, formal interviews, videos and discussion groups. Madden et al., (2013) provide both qualitative and quantitative data consisting of phone surveys, focus groups and questionnaires.

My primary data was collated from a focus group of eight young people aged 13-18, all whom are young people from my extended family or close family friends' children. A semi-structured interviewing format was followed for the focus group discussion.

Naturally, there were some ethical issues approaching young people within my personal network; primarily issues relating to conflicts of interest/researcher's role, informed consent, confidentiality, power and pressure. By their very nature, ethical issues are a complicated conundrum. However the process of reflective practice and reflexivity allowed me to explore the aforementioned issues to avoid distorting the research results due to inadvertent influences from myself and participants. Reflexivity involves making the research method itself a focus of inquiry; it entails the researcher being aware of his own actions/decisions, values, assumptions/preconceptions and how these can affect the research process, the data collection and analysis (Parahoo, 2006).

Conflicts of interest occur when the researcher has multiple roles (e.g., a teacher conducting research on his/her students or doctor on his/her patients) leading to role confusion. I thought carefully about the boundaries of my multiple roles; how they could be broken or maintained and the implications to the power dyadics. It was for this reason and consensual concerns that I chose not to pursue pupils from my school. However unintentionally, I managed to duplicate the same scenario outside the school environment.

Out of respect or not wanting to disappoint or jeopardise our relationship, my participants could have felt unwarranted pressure to participate in the focus group (Bean & Silva, 2010; Phillips, 2010). I also considered that they may not want to disclose all their SNS activities in fear of a breach of confidentiality or may feel embarrassed to do so. Equally they could have been excessively eager to please and evince issues which are not accurate.

To tackle the aforesaid concerns, I made sure that all the participants were fully aware and understood that the focus group was completely voluntary. Moreover, they did not have to participate and equally I would not think unfavourably of them should they wish to decline the offer. Legal guardians were approached (for consent) after participants' acceptance (i.e. to avoid undue pressure).

All participants were assured that their input would be valued (regardless of status) and their views would be respected and not judged. Equally I stressed my commitment to confidentiality and assured all participants that their input will remain anonymous.

A pre-brief via the focus group also reiterated expectations. In addition, the young people were also made aware of their rights to refuse participation and their right to decline any questions (Ross et al., 2010).

On reflection, despite a very successful focus group, it may well have been more appropriate to utilise someone else to facilitate the consent procedures and data collection (Bean & Silva, 2010).

CHAPTER 4: RESULTS AND DISCUSSION

It is worth noting that the data collected from the focus group and the online observation has its limitation due to the relatively small nature of the sample and as such results should not be generalised; however, it does reveal a deeper insight into the ways in which young people utilise social networking sites (SNS) and the perceived benefits to them. Similarly due to practical constraints, participants were recruited from a limited geographic location. It is however debatable whether such a factor would have an unequivocal bearing on the findings as the principles and mechanics of SNS are not confined to geography.

For ease of analysis and to maintain focus on the initial research questions posed, I have categorised my findings under the 3 main areas of focus. Namely; why do young people mass to SNS, What do young people express on these site? And how do these sites enhance or fit into the lives of young people? I have also decided to interweave my findings from my secondary research into my findings from my primary research and when appropriate compare and contrast indentified themes.

Examples of emerging themes from my primary research include online identity formation and management, leisure, information/discovery and friendship maintenance/connectivity. Significantly these same themes emerged from the secondary data and from some of the previous studies we looked at in the literature review.

In the focus group, Facebook was the most popular form of SNS used by young people followed by YouTube, Instagram and Twitter. One young person justified her use of having a Facebook account by saying *"All my friends are on Facebook, so it makes sense to be on there too. I would be kinda weird if I wasn't "*

The type of social media used was very much reliant on what they wished to use it for. Most of the participants confirmed that they had at least 3 different forms of social media profiles and most were synchronized/integrated with each other. For example Twitter may be synchronized with their Facebook (and vice versa). The implication is that media was shared on multiple levels at the identical time.

All the participants confirmed that they started their Facebook and other forms of social media profiles with a network of existing friends or family members (Ito et al. 2008). Collectively they expressed that their online network was just an extension of their offline network and SNS allowed them to remain instantly connected to their friends as they would via a mobile phone. However with the added advantage of low cost; or as one young person puts it *"aren't got no contract phone, just a pay as you go, therefore I can jump on my BB or send a message via Facebook which is cheaper than a call or text."* (BB i.e. Blackberry instant messenger, see appendix A.)

These SNS are immediately accessible via the young peoples' mobile phones and in most cases was the predominant method of accessing SNS; offering instant alerts/update feeds (i.e. log of alerts to users) via collaborative technological features such as *'apps.'* (See appendix A.)Some of the young people confirmed that once connections to their immediate network of friends were exhausted, they looked to extend their network to new friends or associates.

One participant disclosed that he had two Facebook profiles, one for close family and friends and the other for people outside his immediate network. He also disclosed that he used one for his external network to 'sound out' people before he sent a friend request or invited them into his immediate network. Ito et al. (2008) found that young people are almost always associating with people they already know in their offline lives but a small fraction explore interest-driven networks and find information that goes beyond their immediate or local community, such as to connect to peers who share specialised and niche interests. Similarly there are marginalised/isolated young people who may seek support and find kindred spirits online such as young people with disabilities, gay, lesbian, bisexual, or transgendered young people. For such young people, SNS can become *"a place to explore their identities beyond the heterosexual normativity of their everyday lives"* Ito et al. (2008 p 18). However this has a potential intrapersonal risk as outlined by Call and Burrow-Sanchez (2010) citing the works of Wolak et al (2004), whereby such vulnerable groups who use social media to seek contact, support or information regarding their sexual orientation are being targeted by sex offenders.

Below is a list of the dialogues/reasons documented by the participants for using SNS. In some cases I have decided to annotate or furnish further clarity on the meaning of the dialogue, themes or theories indentified.

"It's an easy way to stay in contact with my friends"

"Juicy gossip."

"Using Facebook allow me to stay in contact with my old friends from school. Sometime we arrange online to link up and go out." (NB. College student)

"To meet new friends." Miller et al. (2010; p54) describes this as a typical adolescent issue.

"To meet girls."

"To get 'likes', it makes me feel good about myself and boost my confidence. I'm quite a shy person really but on Facebook I'm more sociable"

Miller et al. (2010 ; p58) says *"The anonymity of online communications thought to provide a shield that protects the teen from negative consequences or repercussions (e.g., rejection) that can occur in face-to-face attempts to form relationships."* However Steyer (2012, p5) expresses his concerns when vulnerable young people define themselves by the 'Like' button or when online comments/feedback becomes unfavourable.

"To stay up to date with what's going on in the world."

"To follow celebrities on Twitter. I prefer Twitter and Instagram, there is too much drama on Facebook, plus Facebook is dead, currently Snapchat is the one, it's the new lick." (Snapchat, see appendix A.)

What is very interesting about the aforementioned comment about Facebook is that Madden et al., (2013 p2) also conducted a focus group discussion in which a not too dissimilar comment was echoed by some of the young people. In his report summary he states *"teens show that they have waning enthusiasm for Facebook, disliking the increasing adult presence, people sharing excessively, and stressful "drama," but they keep using it because participation is an important part of overall teenage socializing".*

"Trolling, being an idiot and causing a bit of mayhem, it's fun and you get jokes".

Trolling is making a deliberately provocative, offensive, cynical or sarcastic online posting/message with the aim of upsetting someone or eliciting/goading an angry response from them. (Linskey 2013). Please see screenshot of an example below from Linskey (2013) available at www.thisisparachute.com/2013/11/trolling/

Whilst the example above is from an adult troller, young people are often engaged in this risky phenomenon. Subsequently, you can be blocked by the user, get a barrage of abuse in return or be reported for harassment to the SNS or to the police. Justice Secretary, Chris

Grayling has recently proposed that the Criminal Justice and Courts Bill be amended to tackle internet trolls whereby they can face up to 2 year in jail. (BBC News 2014). Developmental theorist such as Greenfield (2004) and Subrahmnyan et al. (2006) suggest such aggressive and risk orientated behaviour are typical of adolescent developmental needs.

"To pass the time when I'm bored."

"To relax and forget about everyday problems"

"To liaise with some of my online gaming friends."

This is a typical example of Ito et al. (2008) *"Geeking out"* genre of participation (i.e. specialised knowledge groups).

"Its jokes, oh my days, have you seen some of them vines"

(A Vine is a short 6-10 second looping *video* clip of random stuff; normally very humorous)

"To share pictures, music and videos."

Call and Burrow-Sanchez (2010) spoke of the potential risk of downloading pictures, videos or movies from file-sharing apps/software or unintentionally visiting shared link which then direct you to X rated websites. Linked to this are the threat of sexual solicitation (Guana & Subrahmanyam 2009) and victimization/sexual harassment of girls (i.e. girls being pressured to send inappropriate picture of themselves by their male peers or adults posing as young people online).

"Playing online social media games."

"To feel involved with what's going on with my friend and people my age"

"Using the game apps. on Facebook to play games with my friends like Zynga Poker, Farmville and Mafia Wars. You can also play with people from all over the world; it's like a whole new community attached to Facebook. I sometimes befriend people because they can put me on a higher level in Mafia Wars." (See definition of games in appendix A.)

The two aforementioned comments are strong indicators of social age identity which Leung (2010) articulates as a strong motive for SNS use. It is often referred to age identity gratification whereby ones age group membership and inclusion becomes an important facet and central to who a person is. Leung (2010 p123) says "social age identity is an importance of a person's age group to his/her sense of self".

"If I'm having a bad day or something winds me up I use it to offload."

From the above excerpts there are some apparent themes which are summed up below in the order mentioned by the young people;

Informal social contact / gossip / peer activities (i.e. friendship-driven practice)

Connectivity with friends and family / relationship maintenance

Viewing, creating and sharing information/media/experiences

Leisure / entertainment/ alleviating boredom / escapism

Friending, social recognition/peer acceptance/support

Community, national and global awareness

Meeting members of the opposite sex

Identity formation

The frequency with which participants used SNS and the types of engagement differ considerably. Half the group admitted to checking their SNS via their phones 3-5 times a day (whilst not necessary posting anything).

A participant expressed how she felt that SNS has had an uncontrollable hold over her almost like an addiction. She disclosed how she gets anxious and lost if she fails to log on. She says *"I feel like I'm missing out on stuff"*. Similarly 3 members of the group admitted postings items 2-3 times a day whilst the others activities ranged from 3 to 6 times on a weekly basis.

Madden et al., (2013 p22) reported that the frequency of teen social media use have reached a plateau and three in four teen social media users visit the sites on a daily basis. In their most recent survey they found that 42% of teens visited the sites several times per day. Miller et al. (2010; p51) states *"the importance of peer relationships is reflected by the frequency with which teenagers use the internet for social communication."*

Most significantly, SNS was used by participants to promote and broadcast issues of concern and interest through the medium of video, music, images and text. The participants struggled to be specific to what they express online; however they talked about using Facebook and YouTube to share music, vines and anything of interest. A participant spoke with pride and pleasure about making videos from his phones and posting them online. He acknowledged how good it felt to get compliments and recognition from his peers. This gratification and learning from media production has been acknowledged by the likes of Stern (2008), Ito et al. (2008) and Weber and Mitchell (2008 p43) who states *"young people we observed learn through media production which often exemplifies constructivist notions of learning, a self-motivated learning through play, through trial and error, and through actively engaging with the world. Not only do they acquire technical skills, they also learn to create and critique, developing their own sense of aesthetics and learning goals"*. Ito et al. (2008) refer to this genre of participation as *"messing around"*.

The group spoke at length about pictures on Instagram and Facebook. Most admitted (particularly the girls) that they became anxious when posting a new picture of themselves (in fear of negative feedback) or when they have been tagged in what they deem to be an unflattering picture. Madden et al., (2013 p33) reported 91% of teen share photos often on their profile and states *"Photo sharing is a central function of social media engagement and expression for teens"*.

All the girls in the focus group admitted editing their pictures before posting (Mendelson and Papacharissi, 2010). This pattern of behaviour is very much a gender issue as girls have been shown to have a stronger association with online social media appearance (Stefanone et al. 2011). According to Stefanone et al. girls tended to spend more time managing their profiles and post five times more photos on their Facebook page than boys. This has been recently echoed by the BBC citing the works of Eckler et al. (2014) who found that spending excessive time on Facebook looking at pictures of friends could make you become insecure about your body image.

In general, boys' body dissatisfaction is concerned with a lack of muscle mass whilst girls' centre more on weight and as a result are more likely to develop a desire to be thin (Kirsh 2010, p135). This body dissatisfaction is fuelled by traditional and new media (such as SNS) and reinforces sexual and gender stereotypes.

Edited images of fashion models and celebrities, along with tips and techniques for getting fit or staying dangerously thin are common postings and adverting banners on SNS. Indeed exposure to inappropriate advertising on SNS is one of the many risks that young people have to navigate through (Madden et al. 2013).

Dugan (2014) in the Independent (online) reported that Childline have received more than 10,500 calls and online inquiries from young people (predominately from girls of secondary school age) struggling with food and weight-related anxiety in the last financial year. The charity listed increased pressure caused by social media, the growth of celebrity culture, and the rise of anorexia websites as major contributors.

Inevitably there are gaps in this study, (due to my focus on the perceived benefits of SNS) nevertheless, the results above coupled with the secondary analysis of data is indicative that SNS has equally many associated risks as well as rewards. Nonetheless it has a fundamental role to play in reinforcing young peoples' social connectedness, self esteem, social capital, self imagery, self-efficacy, free will, general life skills and knowledge (Ellison, Steinfield, and Lampe; 2007; Ito et al. 2008).

Moreover by taking ownership of their online identity/space young people achieve a sense of empowerment and accomplishment which reinforces their social identity. As one young man puts it; "*I can be cool online*". One could argue that a young person's social media profile is almost like a traditional hot spot for teens to 'hang out' (such as the shopping centre, youth club or the privacy of their own room); thus creating a private online space for intimacy among friends.

SNS also encourages young people to develop their own interest, pursue a new idea/interest and find others to share that interest with. This is invaluable for young people with unusual interest/hobbies. This sense of connection to others who share your interest, foster a sense of purpose, a sense of wellbeing, a sense of belonging to a community, which is important for young people and their self concept as a group. (Stern, 2008 p113; Parks, 2010 p114 and Leung 2010 p122).

SNS provide the platform for young people to explore evolving identity formation (Stern, 2008 p 113), social status, social norms (within the context of reciprocity) friendship, romance interest, whilst also providing young people with an opportunity to explore and share their interest and other facets of youth culture (Ito et al. 2008) Through peer-based learning it supports and maintain the continuance and extension of learning and self expression and can foster community, national, and global awareness /citizenship.

Regular updates and revision of their social media profiles is also an indicative of an adolescent's developmental need to continuously revise, test and recreate their identities. Miller et al. (2010; p60). In this regard, SNS provides a channel through which adolescents play out Erikson's Identity *versus* Role Confusion stage and practice James Marcia's four statuses of identity crisis: identity diffusion, identity foreclosure, identity moratorium, and identity achievement (Santrock, 2011, p. 384-85). However Buckingham (2008 p3) warns about the feasibility of adolescence as such distinct transitional stages.

One must also think carefully about the degree to which these hastily adopted and disposed identities are actually indicative of a genuine commitment and symbolizes actual development and growth. Equally Steyer (2012 p11-27) expresses his apprehension of the implication for a healthy identity formation when it is played out in such a public arena such as SNS where there are enormous social pressures to project the ideal persona.

CHAPTER 5: CONCLUSION

The goal of this study is to investigate and illuminate the benefits connected to SNS use by young people and to put forth a paradigm for understanding why young people mass to such sites, what they express and how it enhances or fits into their lives.

In this concluding section, we reiterate and summarise some of what we learned from our study in relation to the research questions posed and look at the implications for the future with regards to learning, education, policy makers and public participation.

First and foremost this study found that young people mass to SNS for an array of different reasons, however the importance of peer relationship/friendship, social network, personal self expression, coupled with a strong sense of social identity / social age identity are amongst the most strongest motives for young people prevalent use of SNS. Young people are at a point in their lives whereby these factors are important to them and SNS provides a platform for them to shape and navigate their social environment and explore new interest and forms of self expression/identity. As previously discussed, this sense of connection to others who share your interest, foster a sense of purpose/belonging, a sense of wellbeing, a sense of self; all which support the social capital, personal/social identity and psychological wellbeing hypothesis. Equally with regard to the research question posed on what young people express on SNS, we cannot look at this in isolation without considering the motives for its use because they are both intrinsically linked. And ultimately the motives will dictate what young people express on SNS and equally the perceived benefits. Nonetheless, we are able to generalise the type of expression, such as, peer culture/interest, community engagement/age gratification, representation of personal identity and creativity/new media skills.

This study also found that there are a number of significant benefits associated with the use of SNS including: enhanced learning opportunities; facilitating supportive relationships; identity formation; not to mention the emotional /psychological/social wellbeing of young people. In addition, the strong sense of community cohesion and belonging can promote and maintain confidence and resilience; which in turns aid young people to effectively adapt to change and stressful occurrences.

Whilst this study also acknowledges that the online environment and social media use pose certain challenges and risks associated with contact and contents, it can be argued that any setting for social interaction has some form of innate risk. The current discourse implies that young people are naive when comes to internet use and fails to accept that they are often more affianced, knowledgeable and proactive when it comes to safe and responsible online practices than their adult counterparts.

Furthermore Livingstone & Brake (2010) articulate that online opportunities and risk are inherently linked and that policy attempts to limit risk ultimately will limit online opportunities. Giddens (1991:78) too also implies that *'self-actualisation'* is a social process that would ultimately involve opportunity and risk.

These are also many other additional benefits of SNS use, which due to time/study constraint we are unable to investigate. There is the issue of global/national citizenship or community/civic engagement through fundraising for charity and volunteering for local events (including political events). Political candidates, advocacy and issue-orientated groups are increasingly utilising SNS to push their agenda to the youth population and whilst e-learning frameworks are now incorporated into most educational settings, the use of SNS is rarely utilised. Ito et al. (2013 p6) states *"despite its power to advance learning, many parents, educators, and policymakers perceive new media as a distraction from academic learning, civic engagement, and future opportunity"*. However like Ito el al. (2013), this study has shown that there are many benefits to SNS which can also complement formal classroom learning and have significant implications to the global citizenship agenda and global youth work. The education system and policy makers need to recognise this and consider making interest-driven learning relevant to the national curriculum; thus becoming more youth-centered.

APPENDIX A – GLOSSARY OF KEY TERMS

This glossary provides definitions of many of the terms used in this study.

Apps is short for '*application*' – which is a self-reliant program or software designed to fulfil a specific purpose, especially as downloaded by users of mobile device such as Smartphone or tablet computer.

Blackberry Instant Messenger (BBM) – is a proprietary Internet-based PIN instant messenger and video telephony application included on BlackBerry devices that allows messaging and voicecalls between BlackBerry

Blogging – is the act of posting content on a blog (a Web log or online journal) or posting comments on someone else's blog.

Chatrooms or forums – A designated area on the World Wide Web that allows users to communicate with each other through instant messaging.

Cyber-bullying – is bullying that takes place using electronic technology. Electronic technology includes devices and equipment such as cell phones, computers, and tablets as well as communication tools including social media sites, text messages, chat, and websites

Deindividualization – is a concept of losing one's self-awareness or a sense of selfness in group setting i.e. acquisition of a herd like mentality and/or group norms, when one is incorporated into a group and confronted with arousing external stimulation.

Empirical research – is a way of gaining knowledge by means of direct and indirect observation or experience.

Facebook – is a popular free social networking website that allows registered users to create profiles, upload photos and video, send messages and keep in touch with friends, family and colleagues.

Fan/Group Page – is the only way for entities like businesses, organizations, celebrities, musicians and political figures to represent themselves on Facebook. Unlike a personal Facebook profile, fan pages are visible to everybody on the Internet however group page can be a private members page.

FarmVille – is a farming simulation social network game.

Instant messaging (IM) – is a type of online chat which offers real-time text transmission over the Internet.

Instagram – is a photo and video sharing mobile app that enables its users to share its contents on a variety of social networking platforms, such as Facebook, Twitter etc.

Last FM – is a music recommendation service which helps you discover more music based on the songs you play.

'Like' Button – a feature of Facebook, where users can 'like' contents such as a status update, video or picture.

Mafia Wars – is a multiplayer social network game. In Mafia Wars the gamers play as gangsters building their own mafia community. The players fight other players online and complete tasks to gain rewards and strength in the game.

Microblogging – is a web service such as Twitter that allows the subscriber to broadcast short messages (limited to 140 characters) to other subscribers of the service.

MySpace – is a social networking site with a strong music emphasis that allows its users to create web-pages to interact with other users.

Podcast – an episodic series of audio broadcasting but sometimes could be video that is available on the Internet to download to a portable device or personal computer for later playback)

Pinterest – is a web and mobile application that offers an online visual pinboard.

Reciprocity – refers to responding to a positive action with another positive action.

Sexting – is the act of sending sexually explicit messages or photographs, primarily between mobile phones.

Snapchat – is a messaging application for sharing pictures, short videos, messages and video chat. Friends can view Snaps for up to 10 seconds, and then it disappears from the screen; unless they decide to keep it via a screenshot.

Social media – refers to the technology and online social instruments of communication that allow interactive community based content sharing and collaboration.

Social capital / capital gain – is the benefits and value derived from the cooperation/social connections between individuals and groups.

Social networking sites (SNS) – is the phrase used to describe any community-based Web site that enables users to create public profiles within that Web site and form relationships with other users of the same Web site who may access their profile.

Social identity – is a person's sense of who they are based on their group membership(s).

Thick description – refers to the detailed account of field experiences in which the researcher makes explicit the patterns of cultural and social relationships and puts them in context (Holloway, 1997) The term thick descriptions was first used by Ryle (1949) and later by Geertz (1973).

Twitter – is an online social networking service/site that enables users to send and read short 140-character messages called "tweets".

Tumblr – is a microblogging platform and social networking website

Wikis – is a website or database developed collaboratively by a community of users which allows them to add and edit its content.

YouTube – is a video-sharing website.

Zynga Poker – is an application for the social-networking website Facebook which allows users to simulate playing poker in a social gaming environment. Users enter a casino lobby and can play at any table or join friends for a game.

REFERENCES

ACAPS May 2012. *Qualitative and Quantitative. Research Techniques for Humanitarian Needs Assessment. An Introductory Brief.* Available at: http://www.acaps.org/img/documents/q-qualitative-and-quantitative-research.pdf [Accessed Oct. 2014].

Aoyama, I, & Talbert, T. (2010). Cyberbullying internationally increasing: New challenges in the technology generation. In R. Zheng, J. Burrow-Sanchez, & C. J. Drew (Eds.), *Adolescent online social communication and behavior: Relationship formation on the Internet* (pp. 183-210). Hershey, PA: IGI Global.

BBC News, (2014). Internet trolls face longer sentences. [online] Available at: http://www.bbc.co.uk/news/uk-29678989 [Accessed 31 Oct. 2014].

Briggs, H. (2014). *'Selfie' body image warning issued*. [online] BBC News Health. Available at: http://www.bbc.co.uk/news/health-26952394 [Accessed 1 Nov. 2014].

Bean, S., & Silva, D. S. (2010). Betwixt & between: Peer recruiter proximity in community-based research. *The American Journal of Bioethics,* 10(3), 18–19.

Boyd, D. (2007) "Why Youth (Heart) Social Network Sites: The Role of Networked Publics in Teenage Social Life." *MacArthur Foundation Series on Digital Learning – Youth, Identity, and Digital Media Volume* (ed. David Buckingham). Cambridge, MA: MIT Press.

Boyd, D. M., & Ellison, N. B. (2007). Social network sites: Definition, history, and scholarship. *Journal of Computer-Mediated Communication,* 13(1), article 11. Available at: http://onlinelibrary.wiley.com/doi/10.1111/j.1083-6101.2007.00393.x/pdf [Accessed Oct. 2014].

Boyd, D. (2010). *"Social Network Sites as Networked Publics: Affordances, Dynamics, and Implications."* In *Networked Self: Identity, Community, and Culture on Social Network Sites* (ed. Zizi Papacharissi), pp. 39-58.

Bourdieu, P. (1986). The forms of capital. In J. G. Richardson (Ed.), *Handbook of theory and research for the sociology of education* (pp. 241-258). New York: Greenwood.

Buckingham, D (2008), Introducing Identity . in D Buckingham, ed. , *Youth, Identity and Digital Media,* Cambridge, MA: The MIT Press p. 1-24

Bradford, S. and Cullen, F. (eds) (2012) *Research and Research Methods for Youth Practitioners. Abingdon: Routledge.*

Call, M. E. & Burrow-Sanchez, J. J. (2010). Identifying risk factors and enhancing protective factors to prevent adolescent victimization on the Internet. In Zheng, R., Burrow-Sanchez, J. J. & Drew, C. (Eds.) *Adolescent on-line social communication and behavior: Relationship formation on the Internet.* (pp 152- 163)Hershey, PA: IGI Global.

Corsaro, W, A. 1997. *The Sociology of Childhood*. Thousand Oaks, CA: Pine Forge Press.

Coleman, J. S. (1988). Social capital in the creation of human capital. *The American Journal of Sociology*, 94, 95-120.

Cohen, L., & Manion, L. (1994). *Research methods in education*. (4th ed.) London: Routledge.

Creswell, J.W. (2003) *Research design: qualitative, quantitative, and mixed methods approaches* (2nd Edition),Thousand Oaks, CA: Sage Publications.

Davis, S. H. (2007, April). *Bridging the gap between research and practice: What's good, what's bad, and how can one be sure?* Phi Delta Kappan, 88(8), 569–578.

Denzin, N. K. (1970). *The research act in sociology*. Chicago: Aldine

Deaux, K. (1992). "Personalizing Identity and Socializing Self." Pp. 9-33 in *Social Psychology of Identity and the Self-Concept*, edited by Glynis M. Breakwell. London: Surrey University Press.

Dugan, E. (2014). *Exclusive: Eating disorders soar among teens – and social media is to blame*. [Online] The Independent Online. Available at: http://www.independent.co.uk/life-style/health-and-families/health-news/exclusive-eating-disorders-soar-among-teens--and-social-media-is-to-blame-9085500.html [Accessed 31 Oct. 2014].

Ellison, N., Lampe, C., Steinfield, C., & Vitak, J. (2010). With a little help from my Friends: Social network sites and social capital. In Z. Papacharissi (Ed.), *A networked self: Identity, community and culture on social network sites* (pp. 124-145). New York: Routledge.

Ellison, N. B., Steinfield, C. and Lampe, C. (2007), The Benefits of Facebook "Friends:" Social Capital and College Students' Use of Online Social Network Sites. *Journal of Computer-Mediated Communication,* 12: 1143–1168. Available at: http://onlinelibrary.wiley.com/doi/10.1111/j.1083-6101.2007.00367.x/pdf [Accessed Oct. 2014].

Erikson, E. H. (1968). *Identity, youth, and crisis*. New York: Norton

Erikson, E.H. (1970). Reflections on the dissent of contemporary youth., *International Journal of Psychoanalysis*, 51, 11-22.

Geertz, C. (1973). The interpretation of cultures: Selected essays. New York: Basic Books. Available at https://chairoflogicphiloscult.files.wordpress.com/2013/02/clifford-geertz-the-interpretation-of-cultures.pdf [Accessed Oct. 2014].

Giddens, A. (1991) *Modernity and Self-Identity: Self and Society in the Late Modern Age*. Cambridge: Polity Press.

Greenfield, P. (2004) Developmental considerations for determining appropriate Internet use guidelines for children and adolescents *Applied Developmental Psychology 25 751–762*. Available at: http://www.cdmc.ucla.edu/Published_Research_files/Developmental_considerations.pdf [Accessed Oct. 2014].

Goffman, E. *(1956) The Presentation of Self in Everyday Life*. Edinburgh: University of Edinburgh, Social Sciences Research Centre, Monograph no. 2. Available at: http://monoskop.org/images/1/19/Goffman_Erving_The_Presentation_of_Self_in_Everyday_Life.pdf [Accessed Oct. 2014].

Guana, S. S., & Subrahmanyam, K. (2009).Youth Internet use: risks and opportunities. *Current Opinion in Psychiatry*, 22, 351-356. Available at: http://www.cdmc.ucla.edu/KS_Media_biblio_files/Guan%20%26%20Subrahmanyam%202009_1.pdf[Accessed Oct. 2014].

Harwood, J. (2006). Social identity. In G. Shepherd, J. St. John, & T. Striphas (Eds.), *Communication as Perspectives on theory.* (pp. 84-91). Thousand Oaks, CA: SAGE Publications

Heaton, J. (1998). *Secondary Analysis of qualitative data. Social Research Update* vol. 22. Available at: https://www.esrc.ac.uk/my-esrc/grants/R000222918/outputs/Download/70fef56f-8423-4d20-969e-2cf95bc23f53[Accessed Oct. 2014].

Hitchcock, J. (2008) „Public or private? A social cognitive exploratory study of privacy on social networking sites" in Masters Abstracts International 46(5):2364.

Hinduja, S. and Patching, J., W. (2008) Social networking and identity construction: Personal Information of Adolescents on the Internet: A Quantitative Content Analysis of MySpace', in *Journal of Adolescence* 31 (1), 125-146.

Hinds, P.S., Vogel, R.J., Clarke-Steffen, L. (1997) The possibilities and pitfalls of doing a secondary analysis of a qualitative data set. *Qualitative Health Research.* 7(3): 408-24.

Holloway, I. (1997). *Basic Concepts for Qualitative Research*. London: Blackwell Science.

Invisible Children, (2014). KONY 2012 | *Invisible Children.* [Online] Available at: http://invisiblechildren.com/kony-2012/ [Accessed 5 Oct. 2014].

Ito, M., Horst, H. A., Bittanti, M., Boyd, d., Herr-Stephenson, B., Lange, P. G., et al. (2008). *Living and Learning with New Media: Summary of Findings from the Digital Youth Project.* Chicago: The John D. and Catherine T. MacArthur Foundation. Available at: http://digitalyouth.ischool.berkeley.edu/files/report/digitalyouth-WhitePaper.pdf [Accessed 5 Oct. 2014].

Ito, M., et al. (2009). *Hanging Out, Messing Around, and Geeking Out: Kids Living and Learning with New Media.* Cambridge, MA: MIT Press. Available at: http://mitpress.mit.edu/sites/default/files/titles/free_download/9780262013369_Hanging_Out.pdf [Accessed 5 Oct. 2014].

Ito, M., et al. (2013). *Connected Learning: An Agenda for Research and Design.* Irvine, CA: Digital Media and Learning Research Hub. Available at: http://dmlhub.net/sites/default/files/ConnectedLearning_report.pdf [Accessed 5 Oct. 2014].

James, A. and Prout, A. eds. 1997. Constructing and Reconstructing Childhood: *Contemporary Issues in the Sociological Study of Childhood.* Philadelphia, PA: RoutledgeFarmer.

Kann, M.E., Berry, J., Gant, C. & Zager, P. (2007),*The internet & youth political participation"*, First Monday, 12(8). Available at: http://www.firstmonday.org/ojs/index.php/fm/article/view/1977/1852 [Accessed Oct. 2014].

Kaplan, B. and Duchon, D. (1988). *Combining qualitative and quantitative methods information systems research: a case study.* MISQ, 12 (4), 571-586. Available at: http://business.unr.edu/faculty/kuechler/750/Kaplan%20and%20Douchon.pdf [Accessed Oct. 2014].

King, G., Keohane, R.O., & Verba, S. (1994). *Designing Social Inquiry: Scientific Inference in Qualitative Research.* Princeton, N.J.: Princeton University Press

Kiss, J. (2014). Facebook's 10th birthday: from college dorm to 1.23 billion users. The Guardian. [Online] Available at: http://www.theguardian.com/technology/2014/feb/04/facebook-10-years-mark-zuckerberg [Accessed 5 Oct. 2014].

Kirsh, S. (2010). Media and Youth: A Developmental Perspective. Malden, MA: Wiley-Blackwell.

Kumar R 2012 (3rd ed) *Research methodology: a step –by-step guide for beginners*. Los Angeles: Sage.

Leedy, P. & Ormrod, J. (2001). *Practical research: Planning and design* (7th ed.). Upper Saddle River, NJ: Merrill Prentice Hall. Thousand Oaks: SAGE Publications. p15

Lenhart, A. & Madden, M. (2007) *Social Networking Websites and Teens: An Overview.* Pew Internet and American Life Project, Washington. Available at: http://www.pewinternet.org/files/old-media/Files/Reports/2007/PIP_Teens_Social_Media_Final.pdf.pdf [Accessed Oct. 2014].

Lenhart, A., Rainie, L., & Lewis, O. (2001, June 20).*Teenage life online: The rise of the instant-message generation and the internet's impact on friendships and family relationships.* Washington, DC: Pew Internet and American Life Project. Available at: http://www.pewinternet.org/files/old-media/Files/Reports/2001/PIP_Teens_Report.pdf.pdf [Accessed Oct. 2014].

Lee, A. S. "Integrating Positivist and Interpretive Approaches to Organizational Research," *Organization Science,* (2), 1991, pp. 342-365. Available at: http://www.uta.edu/faculty/richarme/BSAD%206310/Readings/Johnson%20Bond%20Street.pdf [Accessed Oct. 2014].

Leung, L. (2010). Effects of Motives for Internet Use, Aloneness, and Age Identity Gratifications on Online Social Behaviors and Social Support among Adolescents. In Zheng, R., Burrow-Sanchez, J., & Drew, C. (Eds.), *Adolescent Online Social Communication and Behavior: Relationship Formation on the Internet.* Hershey, PA: IGI Global, Inc.

Long-Sutehall, T., Sque, M. and Addington-Hall, J. (2010) Secondary analysis of qualitative data: a valuable method for exploring sensitive issues with an elusive population? *Journal of Research in Nursing.* 16(4): 335-344. Available at: http://www.wlv.ac.uk/media/wlv/pdf/Secondary-analysis-JRN3815531.pdf [Accessed Oct. 2014].

Lin, Ann Chih. 1998. "Bridging Positivist and Interpretivist Approaches to Qualitative Methods." *Policy Studies Journal* 26(1):162-80. Available at: http://faculty.washington.edu/swhiting/pols502/Lin.pdf [Accessed Oct. 2014].

Livingstone, S. (2008) Taking risky opportunities in youthful content creation: teenagers' use of social networking sites for intimacy, privacy and self-expression. *New media & society*, 10 (3).
pp. 393-411 Available at:
http://eprints.lse.ac.uk/27072/1/Taking_risky_opportunities_in_youthful_content_creation_(LSERO).pdf [Accessed Oct. 2014].

Livingstone, S. and Brake, D. R. (2010) *On the rapid rise of social networking sites: new findings and policy implications.* Children and Society, 24 (1). pp. 75-83. Available at: http://core.kmi.open.ac.uk/download/pdf/96378.pdf [Accessed Oct. 2014].

Linskey, C. (2013). *Internet Trolling.* Parachute. [Online] Available at: https://www.thisisparachute.com/2013/11/trolling/ [Accessed 5 Oct. 2014].

Madden, M., Lenhart, A., Cortesi, S., Gasser, U., Duggan, M., Smith, A., & Beaton, M. (2013). *Teens, social media, and privacy.* Pew Research Center's Internet & American Life Project. Available at: http://www.pewinternet.org/2013/05/21/teens-social-media-and-privacy/ [Accessed Oct. 2014].

Madden, M., Lenhart, A., Duggan, M., Cortesi, S., & Gasser, U. (2013). Teens and technology 2013. Pew Research Center's Internet & American Life Project. Available at: http://www.pewinternet.org/2013/03/13/teens-and-technology-2013/ [Accessed Oct. 2014].

Marcia, J. E. (1966) Development and validation of ego identity statuses. *Journal of Personality and Social Psychology*, 3, 551-558.

Marcia, J. E. (1976) Identity six years after: A follow-up study. *Journal of Youth and Adolescence*, 5, 145-160.

Marcia, J. E. (1980) Identity in adolescence. In J. Adelson (Ed.), *Handbook of Adolescent Psychology*. New York: Wiley.

Marshall, G. ed. 1994. *The Concise Oxford Dictionary of Sociology*. Oxford, UK: Oxford University Press.

Mertens, D.M. (2005). Research methods in education and psychology: *Integrating diversity with quantitative and qualitative approaches*. (2nd ed.) Thousand Oaks: Sage

Mendelson, A. and Papacharissi, Z. (2010) 'Look at us: Collective Narcissism in College. In Z. Papacharissi (Ed.), *A networked self: Identity, community and culture on social network sites* (pp. 151-270). New York: Routledge.

Mesch, G. S. (2010). Internet affordances and teens social communication: From diversification to bonding. In Zheng, R., Burrow-Sanchez, J. J. & Drew, C. (Eds.) *Adolescent on-line social communication and behavior: Relationship formation on the Internet*. (pp 152-163) Hershey, PA: IGI Global.

Miller et al. (2010). Connected at any Cost: Adolescent Developmental Needs and Online Relationship Formation. In R. Zheng, J. Burrow-Sanchez, & C. J. Drew (Eds*.), Adolescent online social communication and behavior: Relationship formation on the Internet* (pp. 50-65). Hershey, PA: IGI Global.

O'Keefe, G. S. & Clarke-Pearson, K. (2011). The Impact of Social Media on Children, Adolescents, and Families. *Pediatrics , 127* (4), 800-804. Available at: http://pediatrics.aappublications.org/content/127/4/800.full.pdf+html [Accessed Oct. 2014].

Parks, M. (2010). Social network sites as virtual communities. In Z. Papacharissi (Ed.), *A networked self: Identity, community and culture on social network sites* (pp. 105-120). New York: Routledge.

Parahoo K, ed (2006) *Nursing Research: Principles, processes and issues*. 2nd edition. Palgrave Macmillan, Basingstoke

Phillips, T. (2010). Protecting the subject: PDR and the potential for compromised consent. *The American Journal of Bioethics,* 10(3), 14–15.

Ponterotto, J. G. (2005). Qualitative research in counselling psychology: A primer on research paradigms and philosophy of science. *Journal of Counselling Psychology,* 126-136.

Putnam, R. (2000) *Bowling Alone: The Collapse and Revival of American Community* (New York: Simon and Schuster).

Rise-online.co.uk, (2014). RISE Online - Welcome to RISE. [Online] Available at: http://www.rise-online.co.uk/ [Accessed 30 Oct. 2014].

Rogers, C & Ludhra, G 2012, 'Research ethics: participation, social difference and informed consent'. in S Bradford & F Cullen (eds), *Research and research methods for youth practitioners.* Routledge, London, pp. 43-65.

Roth, Wendy D. and Jal D. Mehta. 2002. "The Rashomon Effect: Combining Positivist and Interpretive Approaches in the Analysis of Contested Events." Sociological Methods and Research, 31(2):131-173. Available at: http://www.sagepub.com/isw6/articles/ch3roth.pdf [Accessed Oct. 2014].

Ross, L., Loup, A., Nelson, R., Botkin, J., Kost, R., Smith, G., & Gehlert, S. (2010). Challenges of collaboration for academic and community partners in a research partnership: Points to consider. *Journal of Empirical Research on Human Research Ethics,* 5(1), 19–31.

Ryle, G. (1949). *The Concept of Mind*. London: Hutchinson.

Santrock, J. W. (2011). *Life-Span Development* (13th ed.). New York: McGraw-Hill.

Smith, A., Lehman Schlozman, K., Verba, Si. & Brady (2009) The internet and civic engagement. PEW Internet and America Life Project, Washington DC. Available at: http://www.pewinternet.org/files/old-media/Files/Reports/2009/The%20Internet%20and%20Civic%20Engagement.pdf [Accessed Oct. 2014].

Stefanone, M. A., Lackaff, D. & Rosen, D. (2011) 'Contingencies of self-worth and social networking site behavior', Cyberpsychology, Behavior, and Social Networking, vol. 14, nos 1–2, pp. 41–51. Available at: http://www.buffalo.edu/content/dam/cas/communication/files/Stefanone/Stefanone_cyberpsych.2011.pdf [Accessed Oct. 2014].

Strath.ac.uk, (2014). *News Releases: Social media pics may lead to negative body images – University of Strathclyde*. [Online] Available at: http://www.strath.ac.uk/press/newsreleases/headline_811121_en.html [Accessed 1 Nov. 2014].

Stern, S. (2008) "Producing Sites, Exploring Identities: Youth Online Authorship." :*Youth, Identity, and Digital Media Volume* (ed. David Buckingham). Cambridge, MA: MIT Press, pp. 95-117.

Streubert, H.J., Carpenter, D.R. (1999) *Qualitative Research in Nursing: Advancing the Humanistic Imperative* (2nd edn). Philadelphia: Lippincott.

Steyer, J.P. (2012) *Talking Back to Facebook The Common Sense Guide to Raising Kids in the Digital Age,* New York: Scribner

Steinfield, C., Ellison, N.B.,&Lampe, C. (2008). Social capital, self-esteem, and use of online social network sites: A longitudinal analysis. *Journal of Applied Developmental Psychology*, 29, 434–445. Available at: https://www.msu.edu/~nellison/Steinfield_Ellison_Lampe(2008).pdf [Accessed Oct. 2014].

Subrahmanyam, K., Šmahel, D., & Greenfield, P. M. (2006). Connecting developmental processes to the Internet: Identity presentation and sexual exploration in online teen chatrooms. Developmental Psychology, 42, 1–12 Available at : http://www.apa.org/pubs/journals/releases/dev-423395.pdf [Accessed Oct. 2014].

Tajfel, H., & Turner, J. C. (1986). The social identity theory of intergroup behaviour. In S. Worchel & W. G. Austin (Eds.), *Psychology of Intergroup Relations* (pp. 7–24). Chicago, IL: Nelson-Hall.

Tajfel, H. (1978). Social categorization, social identity, and social comparison. In H. Tajfel (Ed.), *Differentiation between social groups: Studies in the social psychology of inter-group relations*. (pp. 61-76). London: Academic Press.

United Nations , DEFINITION OF YOUTH [Online] Available at: http://www.un.org/esa/socdev/documents/youth/fact-sheets/youth-definition.pdf [Accessed Oct. 2014].

Valenzuela, S., Park, N. & Kee, K.F. (2009). Is there social capital in a social network site? Facebook use and college students' life satisfaction, trust, and participation. *Journal of Computer-Mediated Communication*, 14(4),875–901. Available at : http://onlinelibrary.wiley.com/doi/10.1111/j.1083-6101.2009.01474.x/pdf [Accessed Oct. 2014].

Waterman, A. S., & Archer, S. L. (1990). A life-span perspective on identity formation: Developments in form, function, and process. In P. B. Baltes, D. L. Featherman, & R. M. Lerner (Eds.), *Life-span development and behavior* (Vol. 10, pp. 29–57). Hillsdale, NJ: Erlbaum.

Watkins, C. (2009). *The young and the digital: What the migration to social network sites, games, and anytime, anywhere media means for our future*. New York: Beacon Press. p62-69

Walther, J.B., Van Der Heide, B., Kim, S.Y., Westerman, D., & Tong, S.T.(2008). *The role of friends' appearance and behavior on evaluations of individuals on Facebook: Are we known by the company we keep?* Human Communication Research, 34, 28–49. Available at: file:///C:/Users/Blossom/Downloads/00b49521e03d7aa41f000000.pdf [Accessed Oct. 2014].

Webb, E. J., Campbell, D. T., Schwartz, R. D., and Sechrest, L. (1966). *Unobtrusive Measures: Nonreactive Measures in the Social Sciences.* Chicago: Rand McNally.

Weber, S. and Mitchell. C (2008) "Imagining, Keyboarding, and Posting Identities: Young People and New Media Technologies." - *Youth, Identity, and Digital Media Volume* (ed. David Buckingham). Cambridge, MA: MIT Press, pp. 25-46.

Wellman, B., Salaff, J., Dimitrova, D., Garton, L., Gulia, M. & Haythornthwaite, C. (1996), *'Computer Networks as Social Networks: Collaborative Work, Telework, and Virtual Community'*,Annu. Rev. Sociol. 22, 213–238. Available at: http://www.itu.dk/stud/speciale/specialeprojekt/Litteratur/Wellman_1996%20-%20computer%20networks%20as%20social%20networks.pdf [Accessed Oct. 2014].

WHO (World Health Organization), *Maternal, newborn, child and adolescent health Health for the world's adolescents* http://www.who.int/maternal_child_adolescent/topics/adolescence/second-decade/en/ [Accessed Oct. 2014].

Wolak, J., Mitchell, K., & Finkelhor, D. (2006). Online victimization of youth : Five years later. *National Center for Missing & Exploited Children Bulletin*(NCMEC 07–06–025). Alexandria, VA: Available at : http://www.unh.edu/ccrc/pdf/CV138.pdf [Accessed Oct. 2014].

Wolak, J., Mitchell, K., & Finkelhor, D. (2004). Internet-initiated sex crimes against minors: Implications for prevention based on findings from a national study. *Journal of Adolescent Health*, 35(5), 424.e411-424.e420.

Wolfe, D. A., Jaffe, P. G., & Crooks, C. V. (2006). *Adolescent risk behaviors: Why teens experiment and strategies to keep them safe.* New Haven, CT: Yale University Press.

Wolak, J., Finkelhor, D., Mitchell, K.J., & Ybarra, M.L. (2008). Online "predators" and victims: Myths, realities and implications for prevention and treatment. *American Psychologist, 63*,(2) 111-128. Available at : http://www.apa.org/pubs/journals/releases/amp-632111.pdf [Accessed Oct. 2014].